Written Pictures
of Life

Written Pictures
of Life

JEFFREY M. RUSSO

iUniverse, Inc.
Bloomington

WRITTEN PICTURES OF LIFE

iUniverse books may be ordered through booksellers or by contacting:

iUniverse
1663 Liberty Drive
Bloomington, IN 47403
www.iuniverse.com
1-800-Authors (1-800-288-4677)

ISBN: 978-1-4620-5325-4 (sc)
ISBN: 978-1-4620-5327-8 (hc)
ISBN: 978-1-4620-5326-1 (ebk)

Printed in the United States of America

iUniverse rev. date: 09/21/2011

For Christina,
without whom life just isn't the same.

My Muse

You're the person
who helped to
change my life.

You're the story
that I hear
in my mind.

You're the vision
that brought color
to my eye.

You're the inspiration
that fully awoke
my creative soul,

so now I
take pen in hand
and begin
to write once again.

The Starlit Sky

I lay down upon
the cool summer lawn,
clasping my hands
behind my head, and
look upward into the
twinkling starlit night

to watch a glimmering
playground before me,
and chuckle softly at
the man on the moon,
then pick out every
constellation I see.

Each planet seems to
shine brighter than the
one before as I hear
the crickets call out
from the trees and
witness a shooting light
flash across the starlit sky.

You

I can already see
within your crystal-blue eyes
your children's lives,
knowing them all
instantly by how
they look just like you.

I sense a strength
in you like no one else
I've ever met,
a joyful humor
that makes even my hardest days
slip away with your smile
and gentle laugh.

Jeffrey M. Russo

The Quiet City at Dawn

I wandered about the sleeping city
and watched as the slow morning sun
rose over the quiet, vacant streets,
not a person in sight,
all the theaters and
bars quite idle and dark.

As I walked, I
noticed a delicate
little flower blooming
from the earth,
and a newspaper
tumbled softly across
the ground; the
still-active traffic lights
flashed between
red and green,
but there were
no cars yet to be seen.

The Rain's Song

It's raining outside.
As I listen to
it fall from the
shaded gray clouds,

it creates a wonderfully
rhythmic sound, when
it taps down upon
the street lights.

It patters across
the puddles on
the road with
its crisp clatter and clap.

It lulls you
to sleep,
its gentle song,
when taking an
early afternoon nap.

Jeffrey M. Russo

A Soft Good-Bye

As I watch you
slowly drive away,
I begin to miss
you already.

How do I muddle
through the months
in your absence?

How do I manage
to make the
time go by?

As I watch your
car disappear in
the distance, tears
spill from my eyes
and I whisper out
a soft good-bye.

Candy-Colored Leaves

Flitter,
flutter,
fall,
one by one the leaves
drop off their trees,
flitter,
flutter,
fall,
to dance blithely about
the clear blue sky.
Flitter,
flutter,
fall,
each candy-colored leaf
tumbles down toward the earth,
flitter,
flutter,
fall,
to dapple
the dark-green lawn.

Jeffrey M. Russo

A Most Likely Destination

The railway warning bell
clamored aloud
as its lights flashed
fluorescent red.

Then a train came
to a halt, on this
dreary fall day
and tiny yellow leaves
floated down from the
trees, gliding over
the great steel cars.

The people who stood
waiting drew open
their umbrellas as
the cold rain blew in,
then hurried aboard
their ride for a
most likely destination.

The Little Pink Bootie

A father held his newborn daughter close,
trying to keep her warm
during his long walk down the hall,
never noticing
her little pink bootie
fall to the floor.

A young girl stood closely behind him
and saw what the father had not;
reaching down quickly,
she picked pick up the infant's little sock.

When she offered him
the little pink bootie in her palm,
he smiled and thanked her.

He thought for a moment
what to do with the sock,
reaching by reflex for his pocket,
and,
with only the tiniest pause,
wryly amused,
sliding the stocking over her little foot.

Missing You

I miss you
when you're gone
so much
that I count the days,
until I have the chance
again to see you.

I miss you
when you're gone
so much
that when I
hear your voice,
my heart beats
faster and my
life becomes new.

I miss you
when you're gone
so much
that with your
return, I know
with time's passage
a dream really
does come true.

A Perfectly Pink Glow

The sunrise came early,
a perfectly pink glow
rising along the horizon,
warming winter's gloomy sky.

The long barren tree limbs
seemed like
a thousand tiny fingertips,
stretching out
to touch its beauty.

Jeffrey M. Russo

The Snow-Covered Evergreen Trees

The soft snow fell
from a pewter sky,
brushed by the breeze
against a row of evergreens,
painting each limb,
riming the dense dark needles
with a glimmering
coat of frosty winter white.

A Swaying Tree Branch

A strong windstorm
rattled the dismal sky,
splitting apart an
old tree branch
that thrashed in the
howling gale outside.

It battered a
quiet home with
repetitive blows,
sounding out with a
thunderous clamor against
the thin walls.

Jeffrey M. Russo

The Frozen Raindrops

The clear frozen
raindrops clung to
the underside of
the trees' outstretched
arms, like time
had fallen suddenly still.

Pure crystal
droplets of ice
glistened in the
cold sunlight

garnishing their limbs
like blissfully hung
pearls spread along
each tree branch on
this frigid morning
of Christmas Eve.

A Perfect Ring of Icicles

The night sky was
black as coal,
no stars in sight,
for all I could see
was a heavy snowfall
swirling by a
glistening lampposts,
solitary ray of light.

The snow touched
the warm surface of the gleaming bulb,
then froze quickly in
the cold snowy air,
slowly forming with
each rolling drop
a perfect ring of
icicles draped around
the lamppost's light.

Again

I'm broken like
an old toy, and
I don't think I
can ever be fixed
again.

I need your help,
I need the sound
of your voice,
I need the joy
of your laughter,
so that I might
be able to smile
again.

I've been hollowed out
like an old tree,
and I can't feel
the thump of my
beating heart.

I need your help,
I need your company
to fill my day,
I need your beauty
to lift my soul,
so that I might
be able to live
again.

Fear

I sit alone
at the hospital,
in an empty
waiting room whose
walls have fallen
too dark to
see, and not
even one person
stands here willing
to support me.

I wait alone
with fear filling
the room, as
my elderly father
fights away death's
reaching grasp
upon a
cold surgical table.

My Quivering Hands

My hands have
begun to shake in
the dawn, with a
lonely, desperate fear.

They tremble beneath
my covers as I
squeeze down tight
to lessen their quiver.

My worries slowly
mount to quietly
muffle my passion
for life.

I may soon break
from this burdensome
weight, as I hope
to speak with someone.

My friends are
not here, for they
are painfully unaware
of my growing despair.

The Cold May Storm

A burst of thunder
shook the sky, and
a pelting cold rain
fell from the clouds.

The bitter chill air
made it feel like
a late November day,
when it was actually
the third of May.

The wind was sharp
and sliced across the
trees, cutting through the
small dead limbs and leaves.

It lashed out against
your body with a force
to knock you back,
and howled aloud like
a caged wild animal.

The storm has raged
for two day now
with no end in sight,
as the wind whips
and whistles about the
city streets, wielding
a cold driving rain.

Jeffrey M. Russo

A Robin's Song

It's just
barely dawn
as a
fresh summer
breeze blows
through my
open window,

while a
robin stirs
me with
its light
sweet song,

I hear
the lyrical
chirps and
whistles flow
from its
beak to
wake me
from a
good night's sleep.

Tender and Hard

A beautiful green-eyed
girl posed
utterly nude in
an abandoned rock
quarry, leaning her
tight lithe body
up against an
immense stone block.

Her delicate pale skin
pressed upon
the coarse stone,
with a comely
shine in the
sunlight, and
as she grasped
at the corners
of the block,
her wonderfully blonde
hair flowed softly
down her back.

Jeffrey M. Russo

The Dry, Scorched Earth

The dry, scorched earth,
cracked along
the lifeless dirt
from the heat
of the blistering sun,
tearing across
the powdery
pale ground,
with deep arid grooves,
in what seemed like
a desperate search for
a heavy quenching rain.

A Restful Night's Sleep

I've returned home
from a long journey,
and my room invites me
with serene silence.

I'm quite exhausted
and my feet are sore,
so I run the water
for a warm bath, then
pull off my clothes,
socks last.

My bed is welcoming
as I collapse upon
the fresh sheets, and
my head finally falls
into the pillow, for
a restful night's sleep.

Sculpted Clowns

A strong-spirited woman
showed me around her home,
bringing me to a favored place
to view her collection of
antique toys and carrousels

We smile and chuckle together
as she turns on their lights,
while I play with her dogs
that are now at my sides.

She holds a genuine love
in her heart that could
brighten the sky on even
the darkest nights.

Then onward we travel,
to a small room filled
with sculpted clowns,
all that you could ever
think to behold, forever
laughing in place.

They were once, long ago,
a favorite of her mother's,
for whom she now graces
only true friends to see.

Waiting

I'm waiting for
a package with
eager excitement,

a package that
holds a dream
fulfilled after
many years of
heartfelt work.

It arrived yesterday
when I wasn't at home,
for there was only a small
note left on the door:

To be delivered
tomorrow between
ten and two,
so here I wait,
sitting patiently
upon my stoop.

Jeffrey M. Russo

I Try to Write and Fail

Write:
please write.
I wish my pen
would stir,
tell me another
story,
sing me another
song.

Write:
my thoughts
have fallen silent,
and my hand
refuses to help—
one word is all
that I need
to begin another
tale.

Write:
please write,
color the sheet
of paper
with a flurry of
newly chosen words.
I seek to find
anything that might
stimulate another
poem.

The Birth of a Poem

A story seeps
into my thoughts,
as words tumble out
from inside my soul.

Words fill an
empty page with incoherent
rhythm, while the poem
in my mind begins
to take form.

Sheets of paper
that may still hold
promise are scratched,
torn, crumpled and
then thrown to the floor.

Images flash and rumble
across my mind,
helping to revise words
that have yet
to make a sound.

I write as fast
as my hand will allow
in telling my tales,
for precision comes later.

Then I'll play with choice
words, and seek their
natural flow, as my story
unfolds from beginning to end.

Jeffrey M. Russo

The Fireflies

The fireflies
glisten across
the hot summer night,
Flittering about
the darkened sky with
A quiet amusement, soaring
together in simple harmony
and twinkling
naturally with
their fluorescent
yellow light.

July Fourth

Listen to the
fireworks crackle and
pop on this
July fourth night,
hear them echo
aloud across the
warm summer sky.

The soft breeze
carries a hint
of smoke and sulfur
over the trees,
and ruffles against
the obscure leaves,

while distant whistles
fly high through
the air, with
their subtle rap-a-tap-taps
bursting everywhere.

Jeffrey M. Russo

One Hundred and Two Degrees

The temperature is
intense as the asphalt
simmers with a haze
in the fierce summer heat.

The air also feels heavy
and is difficult to breathe,
as the fiery rays of
sun burn down against
your skin, reddening
it like a beet.

Nature fights to survive
in the withering sun's
might, for the green
grass and small fauna
slowly die from the
lack of moisture
within the ground.

It wears down upon
your being as you
struggle to cope,
for the city has
become devoid of
people, trying their
best to avoid this
sinister heat.

The Silent Dawn's Light

The silent dawn's light
begins to break through
the dark morning sky,

spreading across the
horizon with a breathtaking
shade of glistening violet.

The glowing array of
colors tears away the
sullen gray clouds,

subtly changing the
night to morning with its
splendid display of light.

Jeffrey M. Russo

The Concert in the Park

I watched the brilliant
orange sun fall below
a distant row of
trees as a throng
of people filled the
inner city park for
the concert here tonight.

A hint of moisture
touched my skin in
the warm summer breeze,
from the old marble
fountains stream of water
trickling gently behind me.

The band began to
sing to all their
fans, and the music
rang from the stage
as the crowd screamed
with sounds of applause.

A massive oak tree
stood tall upon the
center of the park
lawn, with a canopy
of thick green foliage
shadowing us all.

An Alluring Evening Sky

As the sun
fell just below
the horizon, the
evening sky captivated
my eye, with
an alluring aura of radiant pink
and deep blue
colors melding together,

leaving a stark
silhouette of large
evergreen trees at
the forefront of
an open field,
in darkened grandeur.

Jeffrey M. Russo

Trying to Escape Missing You

I woke early, since
your absence
invaded my
sleep, so I rose
up from my bed sheets
and headed to church
to pray before the lord,
then onward
I went toward Cove
Beach to seek a
glorious morning sunrise.

Shortly thereafter I
visited with an old
friend, to share with
him my plight, and
called out to others
hoping to whittle away
more time, only to
hear no reply.

Then I finally reached
the movie theater, trying
to escape missing you
and as the room
went dark, a silent
tear spilled from my
eye, while sitting there
all by myself.

A Collage of Beauty and Light

I want to
color the page
with a collage
of beauty and light,

to paint a
small picture of life
with the ink
inside my pen,

to create an
image of wonder
with a seamless
string of words,

to piece together
a scene in time
with emotions that
truly fill the heart,

to show the
splendor of the moment
with every memorable
story you read.

Jeffrey M. Russo

The Sun's Glory

It was a
perfect start to
a summer day,
as I watched
the sunbeams
shine through the
windswept green
leaves, with splintering
rays of light

that brought out
a subtle tear
from my eye,
as I stood
there alone, awed
with the sun's
glory and graced
by its might.

The Fan on the Floor

It's two thirty
in the morning
and I can't
sleep, for the
pillow is damp
from my sweat
upon its sheet.

A small fan
on the floor,
blows a gentle
breeze across the
sparsely furnished room,
trying to cool
me from this
late summer heat.

Jeffrey M. Russo

The Bright Sunflower

A really large sunflower
grew tall
beside
a tiny old home
whose
lawn had
become very
overgrown. Rising
up toward
the warm
summer sun,
its long bright petals
shined out
amidst the
blue tinted
sky, with
an extremely
lovely yellow.

Gentle Harmony

I wade into the
cool pond, disturbing its
serene calm as the
water ripples around my
waist, and my feet
sink a little into
the muddy earth beneath.

I'm chest deep within
the dark water and
I come to a
sudden halt in silence,
watching the wave of
water I made ease
naturally in gentle harmony.

Jeffrey M. Russo

Standing There

What a gorgeous
summer day it
was for a
picnic, when I
first saw you
standing there with
another girl you
may have just
met, still unsure
of yourself and
the people who
surrounded you. I
caught a glimpse
of your pretty
face and felt
I had to
meet you, so
I approached to
introduce myself and
you shyly spoke,
then turned away
for lack of
words, and I
know now that
was the time
I fell in
love with you.

Dinner for Two

I stand out on
my balcony, watching a
beautiful autumn sunset and
sense a slight hint
of winter in the
breeze, then I feel
her soft warm touch
from behind as she
asks me to come
in from outside to
join her for dinner.

I smile blissfully and
agree, then I follow
her back inside, noticing
a burning piece of
wood, crackling in the
fireplace, so I walk
closer to feel its
warmth upon my face.

I see her shimmering
blue eyes and charming
smile welcome me as
she sits waiting quietly
by the candlelit table,
holding in her delicate
hand a crystal glass
of chilled white wine.

Jeffrey M. Russo

A Little Boy and His Dog

On an early October
afternoon I watched as
a little boy whirled
about a wide open
field, playing with his
baby dog and a
big bouncing red ball.

I saw that the
little boy's parents stood
hand and hand in
the distance, watching the
tender scene unfold between
their young son and
his loving new friend.

Trying to Fall Asleep

I toss and
turn trying to
fall asleep, only
to see the
digital red display
from my clock
gleam out of
the darkness, as
I begin to
think about you.

I wonder how
you're doing, and
hope that your
all right. Or are
you out tonight
having fun with
some friends beneath
the fall moonlight?

I miss you,
that I can't
deny, but I'll
try again to
fall asleep, so
that maybe in
my dreams you
will soon arrive.

I'll Wait

I'll wait,
no matter how
long it takes,
to see you again.

I'll wait
a day to see
your lively smile.

I'll wait
a week to hear
your soft laugh.

I'll wait
a month to sit
by your side.

I'll wait
a year to spend
another day with you.

I'll wait
three years more,
to finally get to
be with you again.

A Beauty beneath a Perfectly Orange Tree

A beautiful woman
strolled beneath a
perfectly orange tree
midway through an
autumn afternoon; her
long boots kicked
about the fallen
leaves and she
wore a long
tweed coat with
a matching beige
scarf and hat.

Her cheeks had
a rosy red
glow from the
wispy cool breeze,
as her blue
eyes glistened in
the sunlight, while
the brilliant orange
leaves fluttered gently
by her side.

The Last Vibrant Rose of Fall

The last
vibrant rose
of fall,
bloomed in
the warm
afternoon sunlight,
beside a
busy street,

Opening fully
for all
to see,
its elegant
royal yellow
and light
pink petals'
colorful majesty.

Your Smile

All the
many wonders
to see
within your
radiant smile,

a smile
with graceful
charm and
wit upon
your face.

a smile
that brings
to light
warm feelings
of life,

causing others
to smile
too, no
matter their
particular mood.

Jeffrey M. Russo

Sometimes Pain Brings Beauty

I'm in pain
'cause I'm afraid,
nervous, and alone.

My heart hurts inside,
feeling I
have no one to talk with.

I'd like to
run from my
life, but I know
I'll never escape.

I miss someone
special to me, a little
more every day, so I try
to keep my thoughts busy.

So I begin
to create beauty
with my words,
that might help my
troubles slip away—

words with light,
words of love,
words about life,
that comes out from
under the pain.

The Beautiful Leaves of Autumn

The splendor of
the autumn leaves
is truly magnificent
to see, when
gazing over the
line of trees.

A fierce, fiery
orange with golden
brown hues, a
splendid yellow shines
with crimson reds
and purples too—

like all the
colors upon a
painter's wooden palette,
before he brushes
them against his
clear white canvas.

Jeffrey M. Russo

Every Day

I see you
every day
in the quiet
of my thoughts.

I feel you
every day
from the depths
of my soul.

I hear you
every day
with the beat
of my heart.

I sense you
every day
in the moments
of my life.

To Dial Your Number

I turn to see my phone
lying upon
the wooden nightstand,

I want
to reach over and
grab it with my hand,

simply to call you
and hear your soothing
soft voice again,

I want
to dial your number
so badly it hurts,
but all I finally do is

wait.

Jeffrey M. Russo

The Wailing Wind

The wailing wind
outside my window,
whips about the
mid-November sky,

possessing a mighty
gust that begins
to make the
old walls creak,

as I listen
to the tumultuous
gale sweep across
the fallen leaves.

Thanksgiving Day

The aroma of
freshly cooked turkey
fills the room, while
the marshmallows
melt over the candied yams,
and
family gathers
happily around
the exquisitely
dressed table.

Pulling forth
their chairs,
sitting together
to eat
and talk
on this fine day,
but first,
their hands join
as a graceful blessing
is
rightfully made.

Jeffrey M. Russo

Another Rainy Day

Winter has arrived
before its timely
date—the
rolling dark clouds
are a dismal
soot gray, on
yet another cold
and rainy day.

I ride through
a deep puddle
with my bike's
rugged tires, and
the cool drops
splash against my
jacket with a
loud chilling splatter.

Ignorance of Love

A heart that is filled with
anger, is
a heart
that has been hurt.

How many times
does a strong heart
have to be
wounded, before
it finally gives out?

Hurtful words
and ignorance
of love
begin to
cleave away
a once loving heart

leaving only
the days ahead,
full
of regret
and empty
lonely lives.

Jeffrey M. Russo

I Don't Know What to Do

I love you
so very much,
for you're the
best part of me.

I'm scared because
I don't know
what to do,
or how I could ever
walk away from you.

I respect you
more than you
know, as a woman
and my friend.

But it just
hurts so much,
when I can't even
talk with you.

I believe with
all my heart,
that we're in
each other's lives
for a reason
maybe not yet seen.

I hold you
in high regard
for the person
you are, but
I just don't know
what to do anymore.

That First Cold Morning

That first cold
morning I'd
step outside my
door, stung
by the temperature.

The warm layers
of clothes I
wore barely
fended away the
crisp chill air.

A cloud of
cold white breath
flowed from my
mouth, as I
felt the moisture
in my nostrils
begin to crack.

My eyes slightly
teared as my
body adjusted to
the cold, and
I heard
the crunch of
the ground beneath
my heavy shoes.

Jeffrey M. Russo

Have You Ever Listened to the Falling Snow?

Falling snow
wafts from the sky with
whispers of light.

A quiet whistle
spirals like a
drifting white cloud.

The wind howls, distant,
and flakes of snow
patter against your skin.

You Fill My Whole Life

You fill
my lungs
with laughter,

you fill
my soul with light,

you fill
my heart
with love,

you fill
my whole
life.

Jeffrey M. Russo

The Right Words

I hope to find
the right words
and the perfect
moonlit evening to
say them on.

I search near
and far for
that precious gift
that may help my
true feelings show.

I yearn to
end my lonely days
with the woman of my dreams,
when she finally falls
in love with me.

Why I Write

Why do I
write? Because
I can't keep all
these words inside.

Like a fire
needs to burn
and a lion
needs to bite,
I write.

I write to
shine a light
on whatever it is
that's on my mind.

I write, words
of beauty or worry,
spilling my feelings
on these blank
sheets of white.

Jeffrey M. Russo

Her Tender Skin

The lamp is low,
the shadows romantic,
as I see her
sensual eyes
glimmer in
the dimness.
Gently, I glide
my fingers
slowly along
the tender curves
of her creamy
white skin.

Little Girl by the Toy Store Window

I saw a little girl
standing by the
toy store window, pressing
her face upon the glass,
marveling over all
the wonderful dolls inside.

I watched as her
warm breath steamed against
the window, hoping to
hold one herself on
Christmas morning, as the
holiday would soon arrive,

only to be startled
a moment later, by
her mother's stern voice,
telling her to hurry,
or they would
soon be late.

Jeffrey M. Russo

There's More Inside of You

I write, only
to see no
reply; I call,
only to hear
your voice on
a machine.
My friends think
I'm a fool who should
walk away from you,
because you're untrue,
but I
don't really want to
for I feel
there's something more
inside of you
that charms me
into loving you.

The First Snowflakes of Winter

The first snowflakes
of winter
were coaxed out
from the cloudy
blue skies of
early December by
the whimsical winds
of nature, and
they swirl softly
about in the icy
air, tiny
flickers of white.

Jeffrey M. Russo

The Birthday Candles

Small
flickering candles,
blown out
with a deep breath,
another
birthday wish
made.

The candles
quietly grow
in number,
as the
birthdays come
and go.

Silently growing
old,
we continue
to blow,
blow, blow,
the years
of our lives
away.

The Christmas Tree Outside

A twinkling display
of decorating lights
were hung upon
the Christmas tree
outside, which caught
my sight while
I rode along
through the cold
dismal night.
They glistened in
reflection against the
silver and gold
balls that shone
so incredibly bright.

Jeffrey M. Russo

Worry, Work, and Hope

I worry about
my parents' health
and when their
hearts might finally
cease to beat.

I head toward
work to escape
my thoughts, even
though my back is
tired and my
feet ache.

I now only
hope for her
speedy arrival, even
if for the
day, so I
can see again
her beautiful face.

Her Perfect Backside

Sharp cold cut short
our conversation—
she turned to her car
with a wry smile good-bye,
leaving me to watch intently
as her perfectly curved backside
swiveled and swayed
down the bustling street.

Jeffrey M. Russo

All My Possessions

Take all my
possessions and sell
my joyful collections,
for they no
longer hold meaning,

spend my money
in any way
you so choose,

but cherish the
stories I wrote,
for they were
the best part
of me, in
my humble honesty.

A Chance to Sleep In

I've been awoken
by the early
morning light.
I lay warm
beneath my flannel
sheets, as I
look over at
my clock and
smile briefly, knowing
that this is
Christmas Day, and
the only gift
I asked for
was the chance
to sleep in.

Jeffrey M. Russo

The Calm before the Storm

It's bitterly cold
outside my window,
and the clouds
are ashen gray.

The barren
tree limbs begin
to sway, in
the rustling wind
from the north,

which brings forth
a massive storm,
in the regrettable
form of snow.

Your Soft, Warm Hand

We're never at
a loss for
words or laughs.
I like when
your soft, warm
hand reaches out,
touching mine, and
our fingers intertwine
at the end
of the night
as I look
into your perfectly
blue eyes, and
say that I'll
love you always.

Jeffrey M. Russo

A Tranquil Blanket of White

After a harsh
winter storm had
passed, the powdery
soft snow covered
a small hillside,
with a perfectly
smooth silver glow.

The tranquil blanket
of white, yet
unblemished to the
eye, sparkled lucidly
in the early
morning light, gracing
all with such
a wonderful sight.

Tired

You lie there
on the couch,
too weary to
climb the steps
toward your bed.

Your tired tiny
body needs its
rest, as your
eyes fight to
stay open, but
finally fall shut.

You've fallen asleep
and your beautiful
face is calm,
with a long
red blanket pulled
nearly to your
nose helping to
keep you warm.

Jeffrey M. Russo

The Full Moon's Glow

The dull morning
sun had yet
to rise into
the early morning
sky, while the
radiant full moon
still lit bright
the cold ebon
dawn with a
luminous glowing light
that reflected upon
the small patches
of ice
dotting the quiet
roadside like shimmering
mirrors of white.

A Wonderful Contrast

It's very late
winter, heavy
snow still covering
mostly everything, and
down from the sky lands a
vibrantly bright red
cardinal with a
flicker of its
soft feathered wings.

It sat
upon an old
broken twig
atop a vast
snow bank of
pure white, resting
for only a
moment, showing off
its wonderful contrast
between color and
light, before flying
back into the
clear blue sky.

Jeffrey M. Russo

Your Calming Voice

I wish
I could
hear your
calming voice,
for as
I listen
to your
kind laugh
or firm
command, even
your subtle
sigh, it
helps to
steer me
from my own dark
anxiety.

Sitting Together

I think the
hardest part of
you not being
here right now

is that I
miss sitting together
over dinner, to
discuss our highs
and lows from
the week, for
hours that we
never feel pass,

or when we're
beside each other,
watching an exciting
movie, or maybe
when we tease
one another during
the scenes that
make us weep.

Sitting with you
is a distinct
pleasure, and clearly
what I miss
most, especially when
we laugh together.

Jeffrey M. Russo

My Strong Loving Embrace

I wrap
my arms
tightly around
you from
behind,
feeling the
tender warmth
of your
skin press
against mine.

I hear
the soft
beat
of your heart
echo
from inside,
knowing that
you feel
safe within
my strong
loving embrace.

Her Snow-Covered Hair

Time grew short
as we tried to
reach our show,
so we ran
through the slick
city streets as
the snow fell.

The cold was
sharp and footing
treacherous, but we
arrived in miraculous
time. We
took off our
coats and started
to get warm,

then I looked
at her,
and saw that
her beautiful blonde
hair adorned with
wind-blown snow,
exuded a sparkling
white glow that
helped to make
a cheerful evening
even more so.

Jeffrey M. Russo

The Last Remnants of Winter

The last remnants
of winter lie
in the shadows,
or where the
weakening beams of
sun only reach
by late afternoon.

Some snow has
been darkened by
earthly filth to
further hinder its
melting, and small
chunks of black
ice still remain.

The gray asphalt
darkens with a
rolling stream of
water, as the
small mounds slowly
drip and trickle
away, while another
brilliant spring awaits.

Becoming Friends

I approached a young
woman at work, whom
I've really only known
in passing, but she
was a charming beauty
and I simply asked
if she would like
to become friends. She
smiled hesitantly since she
hardly knew me herself.

Then she chuckled softly
and agreed, so we
sat atop the small
lounge tables and started
to speak. The
words felt awkward and
unsure at first, but
we slowly began getting
to know each other.

We spoke briefly of
our day and lives,
even about some of
our dreams inside, which
made me happy to
forge a bond that
I hoped would
only continue to grow.

Jeffrey M. Russo

The Earliest of Spring Birds

It's early morning
in late February,
but the long
winter is almost
over. As the
warm rays of
sun shine down
from the pure
blue sky and
the earliest of
spring birds starts
to sing from
out of the
still dormant trees.

The Sounds of the Pouring Rain

I listen
joyfully to
the pouring
rain as
it beats
down musically
against my
window pane.

It's a tranquil
new melody
with each
and every
drop, and
I like
falling asleep
to its
soothing gentle
splashing sound.

Jeffrey M. Russo

Saint Patrick's Day

The pub's doorway
was appropriately dressed
with paper shamrocks,
the beer
had been tinted
green, and emerald
streamers hung down
from the ceiling.

Some of the
Irishmen inside sang
out in brogue,
while others laughed
jubilantly with drinks
in hand, toasting
their shared heritage
with a festive
old Gaelic prayer.

A Lone Purple Tulip

The pearly
white tulips
grew plentifully
by the
side of
an old
maple tree,

but it
took only
a lone
purple tulip,
growing
in their
midst, to
clearly stand
out above
the rest.

Jeffrey M. Russo

Easter Morning Mass

The Easter morning mass
is peaceful and joyous
as the reverend voices
his sermon, and the
brilliant sun shines upon
the pristine stained glass.

The massive altar is
dressed with splendid white
lilies and lilacs, while
the candles' burning light
flickers softly with life.

Droves of people, both
young and old, enter
through every oaken door
to sit or kneel
on their perfectly carved
pews, to pray before
the Lord, for Christ
his son has risen.

A Superb Blue Flower

A superb
blue flower
sprang up
from beneath
a withered
dead lawn,

and reached
out with
its slender
green stem,

toward the
life-giving
light of
the sultry
summer sun.

Jeffrey M. Russo

A Gloomy Morning Fog

A gloomy morning
fog rolled through
the still city
streets, a
thick shroud of
white challenging all
that venture outside,
for they'll
barely be able
to see their
hands, in the
smothering heavy mist.

A Thunderstorm

There's no sound
of pattering rain
outside the window,

but rather a
violent clattering
of thunder as
it rumbles across
the warm sky,

flashes of
lightning electrifying
the ebon night.

Calm Outside

The alarm clock
rings and another
work day begins.
I rise
from my cozy
warm bed with
the brisk morning
dawn, and it
finally seems calm
outside as I
peek out the
window; for the
past several days
there's been nothing
but strong storms
beating furiously down.

Catching My Breath

Like rising from the
depths of water,
I finally catch a
life-saving breath of
crisp fresh air that
soothes my burning lungs.

That's how it truly
feels for me when
I first get to
see your pretty soft
eyes and lovely smile
again, after all the
lonely, hard months apart.

A Part of Me

You're literally a part
of me, an important
piece of the whole
that brightens my soul,
by knowing just how
to make me laugh.

You make me better
than I have any
right to be, from
barbarian to gentleman, or
jester or knight, and
I'd like to thank
you for what your
presence has brought to
every day of my life.

Mothers and Sons

While I stood waiting
for my order at
the local diner, I
saw a young mother
sitting beside her small
son at the corner
booth, eating and laughing
together.

Reaching out, she grasps
his tiny nose between
her forefinger and thumb,
pretending to take his
nose for herself
Watching, I smile from
afar—knowing my mother
played the same
game with me.

Jeffrey M. Russo

Feeding the Swans

We're off to feed
the swans at Holly
Pond, with loaves of
bread purchased solely for
this purpose. As we arrive,
the water is smooth
and calm, few swans in sight, so
we call them, tear
small pieces of
bread and
flick them into the water
with a tiny splash.
Suddenly the swans appear,
gliding effortlessly
across the cool pond
for a floating treat
of fresh wet bread.

Starting to Cherish

The late summer sun
was waning, but not
its heat. I
worked over a hot
grill at the beach,
when a shadow slowly
rose to cover me.

I looked up to
see your steel blue
eyes staring right at
me. I was dirty,
tired and sweaty, but
your cheery smile lifted
me, and your presence
made me feel complete.

We talked and laughed
for a while; as the
activities around us became
a blur, we never
turned from each other.
I'm starting to cherish
you more with every day,
as I know you
cherish me.

Jeffrey M. Russo

The Colors of the Setting Sun

Watch as
the sun seems to set
into the
ocean, and
its profusion
of vivid
colors bursts
against the
darkening clouds
of night,
merging
shadows and
dazzling light.

My Miracle

How could I, at
the lowest point of
my life, meet an
incredible young woman, whose
name starts with the six letters
that spell Christ,
and think that it
was simply by chance?

Knowing this had
to be a sign from
God, to follow along
this path, from
that day forward we've
grown to know, befriend,
and love one another,
creating a lasting relationship
that we'll share forever.

Jeffrey M. Russo

My Love to Write

I really love
to write, and even
if I'm not yet great,
I will continue to try.

I like to try
to build a story,
like others might try
to build a home.

I try to form
an image of color
from what I see
inside of everything.

I try to show
what's inside my heart,
even if it only
agrees with me.

I try to write
a picture of life,
with the words I
choose for everyone to read.